POETRY FROM CRESCENT MOON

William Shakespeare: *The Sonnets*
edited, with an introduction by Mark Tuley

William Shakespeare: *Complete Poems*
edited and introduced by Mark Tuley

Shakespeare: Love, Poetry and Magic in Shakespeare's Sonnets and Plays
by B.D. Barnacle

Edmund Spenser: *Heavenly Love: Selected Poems*
selected and introduced by Teresa Page

Edmund Spenser: *Amoretti*
edited by Teresa Page

Robert Herrick: *Delight In Disorder: Selected Poems*
edited and introduced by M.K. Pace

Sir Thomas Wyatt: *Love For Love: Selected Poems*
selected and introduced by Louise Cooper

John Donne: *Air and Angels: Selected Poems*
selected and introduced by A.H. Ninham

D.H. Lawrence: *Being Alive: Selected Poems*
edited with an introduction by Margaret Elvy

D.H. Lawrence: Symbolic Landscapes
by Jane Foster

D.H. Lawrence: Infinite Sensual Violence
by M.K. Pace

Percy Bysshe Shelley: *Paradise of Golden Lights: Selected Poems*
selected and introduced by Charlotte Greene

Thomas Hardy: *Her Haunting Ground: Selected Poems*
edited, with an introduction by A.H. Ninham

Sexing Hardy: Thomas Hardy and Feminism
by Margaret Elvy

Emily Bronte: *Darkness and Glory: Selected Poems*
selected and introduced by Miriam Chalk

John Keats: *Bright Star: Selected Poems*
edited with an introduction by Miriam Chalk

John Keats: *Poems of 1820*
edited with an introduction by Miriam Chalk

Henry Vaughan: *A Great Ring of Pure and Endless Light: Selected Poems*
selected and introduced by A.H. Ninham

The Crescent Moon Book of Love Poetry
edited by Louise Cooper

The Crescent Moon Book of Mystical Poetry in English
edited by Carol Appleby

The Crescent Moon Book of Nature Poetry From Langland to Lawrence
edited by Margaret Elvy

The Crescent Moon Book of Metaphysical Poetry
edited and introduced by Charlotte Greene

The Crescent Moon Book of Elizabethan Love Poetry
edited and introduced by Carol Appleby

The Crescent Moon Book of Romantic Poetry
edited and introduced by L.M. Poole

Peter Redgrove: Here Comes the Flood
by Jeremy Mark Robinson

Sex-Magic-Poetry-Cornwall: A Flood of Poems
by Peter Redgrove, edited with an essay by Jeremy Mark Robinson

Brigitte's Blue Heart
by Jeremy Reed

Claudia Schiffer's Red Shoes
by Jeremy Reed

By-Blows: Uncollected Poems
by D.J. Enright

Petrarch, Dante and the Troubadours: The Religion of Love and Poetry
by Cassidy Hughes

Dante: *Selections From the Vita Nuova*
translated by Thomas Okey

Arthur Rimbaud: *Selected Poems*
edited and translated by Andrew Jary

Arthur Rimbaud: *A Season in Hell*
edited and translated by Andrew Jary

Rimbaud: Arthur Rimbaud and the Magic of Poetry
by Jeremy Mark Robinson

Friedrich Hölderlin: *Hölderlin's Songs of Light: Selected Poems*
translated by Michael Hamburger

Rainer Maria Rilke: *Dance the Orange:* Selected Poems
translated by Michael Hamburger

Rilke: Space, Essence and Angels in the Poetry of Rainer Maria Rilke
by B.D. Barnacle

German Romantic Poetry: Goethe, Novalis, Heine, Hölderlin
by Carol Appleby

Arseny Tarkovsky: *Life, Life: Selected Poems*
translated by Virginia Rounding

Emily Dickinson: *Wild Nights: Selected Poems*
selected and introduced by Miriam Chalk

Cavafy: Anatomy of a Soul
by Matt Crispin

Diana
by Henry Constable

Delia
by Samuel Daniel

Idea
by Michael Drayton

Astrophil and Stella
by Sir Philip Sidney

Elizabethan Sonnet Cycles
by Daniel, Drayton, Sidney, Spenser and Shakespeare

Air and Angels:
Selected Poems

Air and Angels
Selected Poems

John Donne

Edited by A.H. Ninham

CRESCENT MOON

Crescent Moon Publishing
P.O. Box 1312
Maidstone, Kent
ME14 5XU, U.K.
www.crmoon.com

First published 1994. Second edition 2008. Revised edition 2016.
Introduction © A.H. Ninham, 1994, 2008, 2016.

Printed and bound in the U.S.A..
Set in Garamond Book 12 on 15pt.
Designed by Radiance Graphics.

The right of A.H. Ninham to be identified as the editor of *Selected Poems: Love For Love* has been asserted generally in accordance with sections 77 and 78 of the Copyright, Designs and Patents Act 1988.

All rights reserved. No part of this book may be reprinted or reproduced, stored in a retrieval system, or transmitted, in any form or by any means, electronic, mechanical, photocopying, recording or otherwise, without permission from the publisher.

British Library Cataloguing in Publication data

Donne, John
Love's Alchemy: Selected Poems. - (British Poets Series)
I. Title II. Ninham, A.H.
III. Series
821.3

ISBN-13 9781861711250
ISBN-13 9781861715395

Contents

Song: *Go and Catch a Falling Star*   15
The Primrose   17
Love's Alchemy   19
Air and Angels   20
The Extasie   22
from The Relic   26
from The Prohibition   27
from The Canonization   28
Break of Day   29
The Bait   30
Song: *Sweetest love, I do not go*   32
The Dissolution   34
Negative Love   35
from Elegy: To His Mistress Going to Bed   36
from Ecologue 1613, December 26   37
Epigrams   38
To Mr C.B.   39
The Sun Rising   40
The Indifferent   42
Sonnet: The Token   45
Love's Usury   46
The Triple Fool   47
Love's Infiniteness   48
Love's Growth   50
The Dream   52
Love's Deity   54
from An Anatomy of the World   56
from Holy Sonnets   57
Ascension   58
Sonnet V   59
from *Divine Meditations*   60
Upon the Annunciation and Passion
Falling Upon One Day   62
from The Comparison   64

Illustratons 65
A Note On John Donne 73
Bibliography *81*

John Donne

SONG: *GO, AND CATCH A FALLING STAR*

Go and catch a falling star,
  Get with child a mandrake root,
Tell me, where all past years are,
  Or who cleft the devil's foot,
Teach me to hear mermaids singing,
  Or to keep off envy's stinging,
        And find
        What wind
Serves to advance an honest mind.

If thou born to strange sights,
  Things invisible to see,
Ride ten thousand days and nights,
  Till age snow white hairs on thee,
Thou, when thou return'st, wilt tell me
All strange wonders that befell thee,
        And swear
        No where
Lives a woman true, and fair.

If thou find'st one, let me know,
  Such a pilgrimage were sweet,
Yet do not, I would not go,
  Though at next door we might meet,
Though she were true, when you met her,
And last, till you write your letter,
        Yet she

      Will be
False, ere I come, to two, or three.

THE PRIMROSE

      Upon this primrose hill,
      Where, if heaven would distil
A shower of rain, each several drop might go
To his own primrose, and grow man so;
And where their form, and their infinity
      Make a terrestrial galaxy,
      As the small stars do in the sky:
I walk to find a true love; and I see
That 'tis not a mere woman, that is she,
But must, or more, or less than woman be.

      Yet know I not, which flower
      I wish; a six, or four;
For should my true love less than woman be,
She were scarce anything; and then, should she
Be more than woman, she would get above
      All thought of sex, and think to move
      My heart to study her, not to love;
Both these were monsters; since there must
                             reside
Falsehood in woman, I could more abide,
She were by art, than nature falsified.

      Live primroses then, and thrive
      With thy true number, five;
And women, whom this flower doth represent,
With this mysterious number be content;
Ten is the farthest number; if half ten

>   Belong unto each woman, then
>   Each woman may take half us men;
> Or if this will not serve their turn, since all
> Numbers are odd, or even, and they fall
> First into this, five, women may take us all.

LOVE'S ALCHEMY

Some that have deeper digged love's mine than I,
Say, where his centric happiness doth lie:
      I have loved, and got, and told,
But should I love, get, tell, till I were old,
I should not find that hidden mystery;
      Oh, 'tis impostur all:
And as no chemic yet the elixir got,
      But glorifies his pregnant pot,
      If by the way to him befall
Some odoriferous thing, or medicinal,
  So, lovers dreams a rich and long delight,
  But get a winter-seeming summer's night.

Our ease, our thrift, our honour, and our day,
Shall we, for this vain bubble's shadow pay?
      Ends love in this, that my man,
Can be as happy as I can; if he can
Endure the short scorn of a bridegroom's play?
      That loving wretch that swears,
'Tis not the bodies marry, but her angelic finds,
      Would swear as justly, that he hears,
In that day's rude hoarse minstrelsy, the spheres.
Hope not for mind in women; at their best
  Sweetness and wit, they are but mummy,
                      possessed.

AIR AND ANGELS

Twice or thrice had I loved thee,
Before I knew thy face or name;
So in a voice, so in a shapeless flame,
Angels affect us oft, and worshipped be;
  Still, when, to where thou wert, I came,
Some lovely glorious nothing I did see,
  But since my soul, whose child love is,
Takes limbs of flesh, and else could nothing do,
  More subtle than the parent is
Love must not be, but take a body too,
  And therefore what thou wert, and who
    I bid love ask, and now
That it assume thy body, I allow,
And fix itself in thy lip, eye, and brow.

Whilst thus to ballast love, I thought,
And so more steadily to have gone,
With waves which would sink admiration,
I saw, I had love's pinnace overfraught,
  Every thy hair for love to work upon
Is much too much, some fitter must be sought;
  For, nor in nothing, nor in things
Extreme, and scatt'rings bright, can love in here;
  Then as an angel, face and wings
Of air, not pure as it, yet pure doth wear,
  So thy love may be my love's sphere;
    Just such disparity

As is 'twixt air and angels' purity,
'Twixt women's love, and men's will ever be.

THE EXTASIE

Where, like a pillow on a bed,
   A pregnant bank swelled up, to rest
The violet's reclining head,
   Sat we two, one another's best;

Our hands were firmly cemented
   With a false balm, which thence did spring,
Our eye-beams twisted, and did thread
   Our eyes, upon one double string;

So to' intergraft our hands, as yet
   Was all our means to make us one,
And pictures in our eyes to get
   Was all our propagation.

As 'twixt two equal armies, Fate
   Suspends uncertain victory,
Our souls, (which to advance their state,
   Were gone), hung 'twixt her, and me.

And whilst our souls negotiate there,
   We like sepulchral statues lay;
All day, the same our postures were,
   And we said nothing, all the day.

If any, so by love refined,
   That he soul's language understood,
And by god love were grown all mind,

Within convenient distance stood,

He (though he knew not which soul spake
   Because both meant, both spake the same)
Might thence a new concoction take,
   And part far purer than he came.

This extasie doth unperplex
   (We said) and tell us what we love,
We see by this, it was not sex,
   We see, we saw not what did move:

But as all several souls contain
   Mixture of things, they know not what,
Love, these mixed souls doth mix again,
   And makes both one, each this and that.

A single violet transplant,
   The strength, the colour, and the size,
(All which before was poor, and scant,)
   Redoubles still, and multiplies.

When love, with one another so
   Interinanimates two souls,
That abler soul, which thence doth flow,
   Defects of loneliness controls.

We then, who are this new soul, know,
   Of what we are composed, and made,
For, th' atomies of which we grow,
   Are souls, whom no change can invade.

But O alas, so long, so far
   Our bodies why do we forbear?
They are ours, though they are not we, we are
   The intelligences, they the sphere.

We owe them thanks, because they thus,
   Did us, at first convey,
Yielded their forces, sense, to us,
   Nor are dross to us, but allay.

On man heaven's influences works not so,
   But that it first imprints the air,
So soul into the soul may flow,
   Though it to body first repair.

As our blood labours to beget
   Spirits, as like souls as it can,
Because such fingers need to knit
   That subtle knot, which makes us man:

So must pure lovers' souls descend
   T' affections, and to faculties,
Which sense may reach and apprehend,
   Else a great prince in prison lies.

To our bodies turn we then, that so
   Weak men on love revealed may look;
Love's mysteries in souls do grow,
   But yet the body is his book.

And if some lover, such as we,
   Have heard this dialogue of one,

Let him still mark us, he shall see
  Small change, when we' are to bodies gone.

from THE RELIC

      First, we loved well and faithfully,
      Yet knew not what we loved, nor why,
      Difference of sex no more we knew,
      Than our guardian angels do;
          Coming and going, we
Perchance might kiss, but not between those meals;
          Our hands ne'er touched the seals,
Which nature, injured by late law, sets free:
These miracles we did; but now alas,
All measure, and all language, I should pass,
Should I tell what a miracle she was.

from THE PROHIBITION

    Yet, love and hate me too,
So, these extremes shall neither's office do;
    Love me, that I may die the gentler way;
Hate me, because thy love's too great for me;
    Or let these two, themselves, not me decay;
So shall I live thy stage, nor triumph be;
    Lest thou my love and hate and me undo,
    To let me live, Oh love and hate me too.

from THE CANONIZATION

Call us what you will, we are made such by love;
   Call her one, me another fly,
We are tapers too, and at our own cost die,
   And we in us find the eagle and the dove,
     The phoenix riddle hath more wit
     By us; we two being one, are it.
So to one neutral thing both sexes fit
   We die and rise the same, and prove
   Mysterious by this love.

BREAK OF DAY

'Tis true, 'tis day, what though it be?
O wilt thou therefore rise from me?
Why should we rise, because 'tis light?
Did we lie down, because 'twas night?
Love which in spite of darkness brought us hither,
Should in despite of light keep us together.

Light hath no tongue, but is all eye;
If it could speak as well as spy,
This were the worst, that it could say,
That being well, I fain would stay,
And that I loved my heart and honour so,
That I would not from him, that had them, go.

Must business thee from hence remove?
Oh, that's the worst disease of love,
The poor, the foul, the false, love can
Admit but not the busied man.
He which hath business, and makes love, doth do
Such wrong, as when a married man doth won.

THE BAIT

Come live with me, and be my love,
And we will some new pleasures prove
Of golden sands, and crystal brooks,
With silken lines, and silver hooks.

There will the river whispering run
Warmed by thy eyes, more than the sun.
And there the' enamoured fish will stay,
Begging themselves they may betray.

When thou wilt swim in that live bath,
Each fish, which every channel hath,
Will amorously to thee swim,
Gladder to catch thee, than thou him.

If thou, to be so seen, be'st loth,
By sun, or moon, thou darkenest both,
And if myself have leave to see,
I need not their light, having thee.

Lets others freeze with angling reeds,
And cut their legs, with shells and weeds,
Or treacherously poor fish beset,
With strangling snare, or windowy net:

Let coarse bold hands, from slimy nest
The bedded fish in banks out-wrest,
Or curious traitors, sleavesilk flies

Bewitch poor fishes' wandering eyes.

For thee, thou need'st no such deceit,
For thou thyself art thine own bait,
That fish, that is not catched thereby,
Alas, is wiser far than I.

SONG; *SWEETEST LOVE, I DO NOT GO*

Sweetest love, I do not go,
  For weariness of thee,
Nor in hope the world can show
  A fitter love for me;
    But since that I
Must die at last, 'tis best,
To use my self in jest
  Thus by feigned deaths to die.

Yesternight the sun went hence,
  And yet is here today,
He hath no desire nor sense,
  Nor half so short a way:
    Then fear not me,
But believe that I shall make
Speedier journeys, since I take
  More wings and spurs than he.

O how feeble is man's power,
  That if good fortune fall,
Cannot add another hour,
  Nor a lost hour recall!
    But come bad chance,
And we join to it our strength,
And we teach it art and length,

Itself o'er us to advance.

When thou sigh'st, thou sigh'st not wind,
  But sigh'st my soul away,
When thou weep'st, unkindly kind,
  My life's blood doth decay.
    It cannot be
That thou lov'st me, as thou say'st,
If in thine my life thou waste,
  Thou art the best of me.

Let not thy diving heart
  Forethink me any ill,
Destiny may take thy part,
  And may thy fears fulfil;
    But think that we
Are but turned aside to sleep;
They who one another keep
  Alive, n'er parted be.

THE DISSOLUTION

She is dead; and all which die
  To their first elements resolve;
And we were mutual elements to us,
    And made of one another.
  My body then doth hers involve,
And those things whereof I consist, hereby
In me abundant grow, and burdenous,
    And nourish not, but smother.
  My fire of passion, sighs of air,
Water of tears, and earthy sad despair,
      Which my materials be,
But near worn out by love's security,
She, to my loss, doth by her death repair,
  And I might live long wretched so
But that my fire doth with my fuel grow.
    Now as those active kings
  Whose foreign conquest treasure brings,
Receive more, and spend more, and soonest break:
This (which I amazed that I can speak)
    This death, hath with my store
      My use increased.
And so my soul more earnestly released,
Will outstrip hers; as bullets flown before
A latter bullet may o'ertake, the powder being more.

NEGATIVE LOVE

I never stooped so low, as they
Which on an eye, cheek, lip, can prey,
   Seldom to them, which soar no higher
   Than virtue or the mind to admire,
For sense, and understanding may
   Know, what gives fuel to their fire:
My love, though silly, is more brave,
For may I miss, whene'er I crave,
If I know yet what I would have,.

If that be simply perfectest
Which can by no way be expressed
   But negatives, my love is so.
   To all, which all love, I say no.
If any who decipher best,
   What we know not, ourselves, can know,
Let him teach me that nothing; this
As yet my ease, and comfort is,
Though I speed not, I cannot miss.

ELEGY: TO HIS MISTRESS GOING TO BED

Come, Madam, come, all rest my powers defie,
 Until I labour, I in labour lie.
The foe oft-times having the foe in sight,
Is tir'd with standing though he never fight.

Off with that girdle, like heavens Zone glittering,
But a far fairer world incompassing.
Unpin that spangled breastplate which you wear,
That th'eyes of busie fooles may be stopt there.
Unlace your self, for that harmonious chyme,

Tells me from you, that now it is bed time.
Off with that happy busk, which I envie,
That still can be, and still can stand so nigh.
Your gown going off, such beautious state reveals,
As when from flowry meads th'hills shadow steales.

Off with that wyerie Coronet and shew
The haiery Diademe which on you doth grow:
Now off with those shooes, and then safely tread
In this loves hallow'd temple, this soft bed.
In such white robes, heaven's Angels us'd to be

Receavd by men; Thou Angel bringst with thee
A heaven like Mahomets Paradise; and though
Ill spirits walk in white, we easly know,
By this these Angels from an evil sprite,

Those set our hairs, but these our flesh upright.

Licence my roaving hands, and let them go,
Before, behind, between, above, below.
O my America! my new-found-land,
My kingdome, safliest when with one man man'd,
My Myne of precious stones, My Emperie,

How blest am I in this discovering thee!
To enter in these bonds, is to be free;
Then where my hand is set, my seal shall be.
Full nakedness! All joyes are due to thee,
As souls unbodied, bodies uncloth'd must be,

To taste whole joyes. Gems which you women use
Are like Atlanta's balls, cast in mens views,
That when a fools eye lighteth on a Gem,
His earthly soul may covet theirs, not them.
Like pictures, or like books gay coverings made

For lay-men, are all women thus array'd;
Themselves are mystick books, which only wee
(Whom their imputed grace will dignifie)
Must see reveal'd. Then since that I may know;
As liberally, as to a Midwife, shew

Thy self: cast all, yea, this white lynnen hence,
There is no pennance due to innocence.
To teach thee, I am naked first; why than
What needst thou have more covering then a man.

from ECOLOGUE 1613. DECEMBER 26

The Benediction

Blessed pair of swans, oh may you interbring
    Daily new joys, and never sing,
    Live, till all grounds of wishes fail,
Til honour, yea till wisdom grow so stale,
    That, new great heights to try,
It must serve your ambition, to die;
Raise heirs, and may here, to the world's end, live
Heirs from this King, to take thanks, yours, to give,
Nature and grace do all, and nothing art,
Ay never age, or error overthwart
With any west, these radiant eyes, with any
        north, this heart.

EPIGRAMS

HERO AND LEANDER

Both robbed of Air, we both lie in ground,
Both whom one fire had burnt, one water drowned.

MANLINESS

Thou call'st me effeminate, for I love women's joys;
I call not thee manly, though thou follow boys.

TO MR C.B.

Thy friend, whom thy deserts to thee enchain,
  Urged by this inexcusable occasion,
  Thee and the saint of his affection
Leaving behind, doth of both wants complain;
And let the love I bear to both sustain
  No blot nor maim by this division,
Strong is this love which ties our hearts in one,
And strong that love pursued with amorous pain;
But though besides thyself I leave behind
  Heaven's liberal, and earth's thrice-fairer sun,
  Going to where stern winter aye doth won,
Yet, love's hot fires, which martyr my sad mind,
  Do send forth scalding sighs, which have the art
  To melt all ice, but that which walls her heart.

THE SUN RISING

    Busie old foole, unruly Sunne,
      Why dost thou thus,
Through windowes, and through curtaines call on us?
Must to thy motions lovers seasons run?
     Sawcy pedantique wretch, goe chide
     Late schoole boyes, and sowre prentices,
   Goe tell Court-huntsmen, that the King will ride,
   Call countrey ants to harvest offices;
Love, all alike, no season knowes, nor clyme,
Nor houres, dayes, moneths, which are the rags of time.

    Thy beames, so reverend, and strong
      Why shouldst thou thinke?
I could eclipse and cloud them with a winke,
But that I would not lose her sight so long:
     If her eyes have not blinded thine,
     Looke, and to morrow late, tell mee,
   Whether both the'India's of spice and Myne
   Be where thou leftst them, or lie here with mee.
Aske for those Kings whom thou saw'st yesterday,
And thou shalt heare, All here in one bed lay.

    She'is all States, and all Princes, I,
      Nothing else is.
Princes doe but play us; compar'd to this,
All honor's mimique; All wealth alchimie.
     Thou sunne art halfe as happy'as wee,
     In that the world's contracted thus;

    Thine age askes ease, and since thy duties bee
      To warme the world, that's done in warming us.
Shine here to us, and thou art every where;
This bed thy center is, these walls, thy spheare.

THE INDIFFERENT

I can love both faire and browne,
 Her whom abundance melts, and her whom want
                                    betraies,
Her who loves lonenesse best, and her who maskes and
                                      plaies,
Her whom the country form'd, and whom the town,
Her who beleeves, and her who tries,
Her who still weepes with spungie eyes,
And her who is dry corke, and never cries;
I can love her, and her, and you and you,
I can love any, so she be not true.

Will no other vice content you?
Wil it not serve your turn to do, as did your mothers?
Or have you all old vices spent, and now would finde
                                    out others?
Or doth a feare, that men are true, torment you?
Oh we are not, be not you so,
Let mee, and doe you, twenty know.
Rob mee, but binde me not, and let me goe.
Must I, who came to travaile thorow you,
Grow your fixt subject, because you are true?

Venus heard me sigh this song,
And by Loves sweetest Part, Variety, she swore,
She heard not this till now; and that it should be so no
                                      more.
She went, examin'd, and return'd ere long,

And said, alas, Some two or three
Poore Heretiques in love there bee,
Which thinke to stablish dangerous constancie.
But I have told them, since you will be true,
You shall be true to them, who'are false to you.

SONNET: THE TOKEN

Send me some token, that my hope may live,
   Or that my easelesse thoughts may sleep and rest;
Send me some honey to make sweet my hive,
   That in my passion I may hope the best.
I beg noe ribbond wrought with thine owne hands,
   To knit our loves in the fantastick straine
Of new-toucht youth; nor Ring to shew the stands
   Of our affection, that as that's round and plaine,
So should our loves meet in simplicity;
   No, nor the Coralls which thy wrist infold,
Lac'd up together in congruity,
   To shew our thoughts should rest in the same hold;
No, nor thy picture, though most gracious,
   And most desir'd, because best like the best;
Nor witty Lines, which are most copious,
   Within the Writings which thou hast addrest.
Send me nor this, nor that, t'increase my store,
But swear thou thinkst I love thee, and no more.

LOVE'S USURY

For every houre that thou wilt spare mee now,
        I will allow,
Usurious God of Love, twenty to thee,
When with my browne, my gray haires equall bee;
Till then, Love, let my body raigne, and let
Mee travell, sojourne, snatch, plot, have, forget,
Resume my last yeares relict: thinke that yet
        We'had never met.

Let mee thinke any rivalls letter mine,
        And at next nine
Keepe midnights promise; mistake by the way
The maid, and tell the Lady of that delay;
Onely let mee love none, no, not the sport;
From country grasse, to comfitures of Court,
Or cities quelque choses, let report
        My minde transport.

This bargaine's good; if when I'am old, I bee
        Inflam'd by thee,
If thine owne honour, or my shame, or paine,
Thou covet most, at that age thou shalt gaine.
Doe thy will then, then subject and degree,
And fruit of love, Love I submit to thee,
Spare mee till then, I'll beare it, though she bee
        One that loves mee.

THE TRIPLE FOOL

    I am two fooles, I know,
      For loving, and for saying so
         In whining Poëtry;
But where's that wiseman, that would not be I,
      If she would not deny?
Then as th'earths inward narrow crooked lanes
    Do purge sea waters fretfull salt away,
I thought, if I could draw my paines,
    Through Rimes vexation, I should them allay,
Griefe brought to numbers cannot be so fierce,
For, he tames it, that fetters it in verse.

    But when I have done so,
      Some man, his art and voice to show,
         Doth Set and sing my paine,
And, by delighting many, frees againe
    Griefe, which verse did restraine.
To Love, and Griefe tribute of Verse belongs,
    But not of such as pleases when'tis read,
Both are increased by such songs:
    For both their triumphs so are published,
And I, which was two fooles, do so grow three;
Who are a little wise, the best fooles bee.

LOVE'S INFINITENESS

If yet I have not all thy love,
Deare, I shall never have it all,
I cannot breath one other sigh, to move,
Nor can intreat one other teare to fall,
And all my treasure, which should purchase thee,
Sighs, teares, and oathes, and letters I have spent.
Yet no more can be due to mee,
Then at the bargaine made was ment,
If then thy gift of love were partiall,
That some to mee, some should to others fall,
    Deare, I shall never have Thee All.

Or if then thou gavest mee all,
All was but All, which thou hadst then;
But if in thy heart, since, there be or shall,
New love created bee, by other men,
Which have their stocks intire, and can in teares,
In sighs, in oathes, and letters outbid mee,
This new love may beget new feares,
For, this love was not vowed by thee.
And yet it was, thy gift being generall,
The ground, thy heart is mine, what ever shall
    Grow there, deare, I should have it all.

Yet I would not have all yet,
Hee that hath all can have no more,
And since my love doth every day admit
New growth, thou shouldst have new rewards in store;

Thou canst not every day give me thy heart,
If thou canst give it, then thou never gavest it:
Loves riddles are, that though thy heart depart,
It stayes at home, and thou with losing savest it:
But wee will have a way more liberall,
Then changing hearts, to joyne them, so wee shall
   Be one, and one anothers All.

LOVE'S GROWTH

I scarce beleeve my love to be so pure
    As I had thought it was,
    Because it doth endure
Vicissitude, and season, as the grasse;
 Me thinkes I lyed all winter, when I swore,
My love was infinite, if spring make'it more.

But if this medicine, love, which cures all sorrow
With more, not onely bee no quintessence,
But mixt of all stuffes, paining soule, or sense,
And of the Sunne his working vigour borrow,
Love's not so pure, and abstract, as they use
To say, which have no Mistresse but their Muse,
But as all else, being elemented too,
Love sometimes would contemplate, sometimes do.

And yet no greater, but more eminent,
    Love by the spring is growne;
    As, in the firmament,
Starres by the Sunne are not inlarg'd, but showne.
Gentle love deeds, as blossomes on a bough,
From loves awakened root do bud out now.

If, as in water stir'd more circles bee
Produc'd by one, love such additions take,
Those like so many spheares, but one heaven make,
For, they are all concentrique unto thee.
And though each spring doe adde to love new heate,

As princes doe in times of action get
New taxes, and remit them not in peace,
No winter shall abate the springs encrease.

THE DREAM

    Deare love, for nothing lesse then thee
Would I have broke this happy dreame,
        It was a theame
For reason, much too strong for phantasie,
Therefore thou wakd'st me wisely; yet
My Dreame thou brok'st not, but continued'st it,
Thou art so truth, that thoughts of thee suffice,
To make dreames truths; and fables histories;
Enter these armes, for since thou thoughtst it best,
Not to dreame all my dreame, let's act the rest.

    As lightning, or a Tapers light,
Thine eyes, and not thy noise wak'd mee;
        Yet I thought thee
(For thou lovest truth) an Angell, at first sight,
But when I saw thou sawest my heart,
And knew'st my thoughts, beyond an Angels art,
When thou knew'st what I dreamt, when thou knew'st when
Excesse of joy would wake me, and cam'st then,
I must confesse, it could not chuse but bee
Prophane, to thinke thee any thing but thee.

    Comming and staying show'd thee, thee,
But rising makes me doubt, that now,
        Thou art not thou.
That love is weake, where feare's as strong as hee;
'Tis not all spirit, pure, and brave,

If mixture it of *Feare*, *Shame*, *Honor*, have.
Perchance as torches which must ready bee,
Men light and put out, so thou deal'st with mee,
Thou cam'st to kindle, goest to come; Then I
Will dreame that hope againe, but else would die.

LOVE'S DEITY

I long to talke with some old lovers ghost,
   Who dyed before the god of Love was borne:
I cannot thinke that hee, who then lov'd most,
   Sunke so low, as to love one which did scorne.
But since this god produc'd a destinie,
And that vice-nature, custome, lets it be;
   I must love her, that loves not mee.

Sure, they which made him god, meant not so much,
   Nor he, in his young godhead practis'd it;
But when an even flame two hearts did touch,
   His office was indulgently to fit
Actives to passives. Correspondencie
Only his subject was; It cannot bee
   Love, till I love her, that loves mee.

But every moderne god will now extend
   His vast prerogative, as far as Jove.
To rage, to lust, to write to, to commend,
   All is the purlewe of the God of Love.
Oh were wee wak'ned by this Tyrannie
To ungod this child againe, it could not bee
   I should love her, who loves not mee.

Rebell and Atheist too, why murmure I,
   As though I felt the worst that love could doe?
Love might make me leave loving, or might trie
   A deeper plague, to make her love mee too,

Which, since she loves before, I'am loth to see;
Falshood is worse then hate; and that must bee,
   If shee whom I love, should love mee.

from AN ANATOMY OF THE WORLD

She, she is dead; she's dead: when thou know'st this,
Thou know'st how poor a trifling thing man is.
And learn'st thus much by our anatomy,
The heart being perished, no part can be free.
And that except thou feed (not banquet) on
The supernatural food, religion,
Thy better growth grows withered, and scant;
Be more than man, or tho' art less an ant.

from HOLY SONNETS

ANNUNCIATION

Salvation to all that will is nigh,
That all, which always is all everywhere,
Which cannot sin, and yet all sins must bear,
Which cannot die, yet cannot choose but die,
Lo, faithful virgin, yields himself to lie
In prison, in thy womb; and though he there
Can take no sin, nor thou give, yet he 'will wear
Taken from thence, flesh, which death's force may try.
Ere by the spheres time was created, thou
Wast in his mind, who is thy son, and brother,
Whom thou conceiv'st, conceived' yea thou art now
Thy maker's maker, and thy father's mother,
Tho' hast light in dark; and shutt'st in little room,
Immensity cloistered in thy dear womb.

ASCENSION

Salute the last and everlasting day,
Joy at the uprising of this sun, and son,
Ye whose just tears, or tribulation
Have purely washed, or burnt your drossy clay;
Behold the highest, parting hence away,
Lightens the dark clouds, which he treads upon,
Nor doth he by ascending, show alone,
But first he, and he first enters the way.
O strong ram, which hast battered heaven for me,
Mild lamb, which with thy blood, hast marked the path;
Bright torch, which shin'st, that I the way may see,
Oh, with thine own blood quench thine own just wrath,
And if thy holy Spirit, my Muse did raise,
Deign at my hands this crown of prayer and praise.

V

I am a little world made cunningly
Of Elements, and an Angelike spright,
But black sinne hath betraid to endlesse night
My worlds both parts, and (oh) both parts must die.
You which beyond that heaven which was most high
Have found new sphears, and of new lands can write,
Powre new seas in mine eyes, that so I might
Drowne my world with my weeping earnestly,
Or wash it, if it must be drown'd no more:
But oh it must be burnt! alas the fire
Of lust and envie have burnt it heretofore,
And made it fouler; Let their flames retire,
And burne me ô Lord, with a fiery zeale
Of thee and thy house, which doth in eating heale.

from DIVINE MEDITATIONS

1

I am a little world made cunningly
Of elements, and an angelic sprite,
But black sin hath betrayed to endless night
My world's both parts, and, oh, both parts must die.
You which beyond that heaven which was most high
Have found new spheres, and of new lands can write,
Pour news seas in mine eyes, that so I might
Drown my world with my weeping earnestly,
Or wish it if it must be drowned no more:
But oh it must be burnt; alas the fire
Of lust and envy have burnt it heretofore,
And made it fouler; let their flames retire,
And burn me O Lord, with a fiery zeal
Of thee and thy house, which doth in eating heal.

7

At the round earth's imagined corners, blow
Your trumpets, angels, and arise, arise
From death, you numberless infinities
Of souls, and to your scattered bodies go,
All whom the flood did, and fire shall o'erthrow,
All whom war, earth, age, agues, tyrannies,
Despair, law, chance, hath slain, and you whose eyes,
Shall behold God, and never taste death's woe.
But let them sleep, Lord, and me mourn a space,
For, if above all these, my sins abound,
'Tis late to ask abundance of thy grace,
When we are there' here on this lowly ground,
Teach me how to repent; for that's as good
As if thou hadst sealed my pardon, with thy blood.

UPON THE ANNUNCIATION AND PASSION FALLING UPON ONE DAY. 1608

Tamely, frail body' abstain today; today
My soul eats twice, Christ hither and away.
She sees him man, so like God made in this,
That of them both a circle emblem is,
Whose first and last concur; this doubtful day
Of feast or fast, Christ came, and went away;
She sees him nothing twice at once, who is all;
She sees a cedar plant itself, and fall,
Her maker put to making, and the head
Of life, at once, not yet alive, and dead;
She sees at once the virgin mother stay
Reclused at home, public at Golgotha.
Sad and rejoiced she 's seen at once, and seen
At almost fifty, and at scarce fifteen.
At once a son is promised her, and gone,
Gabriel gives Christ to her, he her to John;
Not fully a mother, she's in orbity,
At once receiver and the legacy;
All this, and all between, this day hath shown,
Th' abridgement of Christ's story, which makes one
(As in plain maps, the furthest west is east)
Of the angels' *Ave*, 'and *Consummatum est*.
How well the Church, God's court of faculties
Deals, in some times, and seldom joining these;
As by the self-fixed pole we never do
Direct our course, but the next star thereto,

Which shows where the'other is, and which we say
(Because it strays not far) doth never stray;
So God by his church, nearest to him, we know,
And stand firm, if we by her motion go;
His Spirit, as his fiery pillar doth
Lead, and his church, as cloud; to one end both:
This Church, by letting these days join, hath shown
Death and conception in mankind is one.
Or 'twas in him the same humility,
That he would be a man, and leave to be:
Or as creation he had made, as God,
With the last judgement, but one period,
His imitating spouse would join in one
Manhood's extremes: he shall come, he is gone:
Or as though one blood drop, which thence did fall,
Accepted, would have served, he yet shed all;
So though the least of his pains, deeds, or words,
Would busy a life, she all this day affords;
This treasure then, in gross, my soul unplay,
And in my life retail it every day.

from THE COMPARISON

As the sweet sweet of roses in a still,
As that which from chafed musk cat's pores doth trill,
As the almighty balm of th' early east,
Such as the sweat drops of my mistress' breast.
And on her neck her skin such lustre sets,
They seem no sweat drops, but pearl carcanets. Rank
sweaty froth thy mistress' brow defiles,
Like spermatic issue of ripe menstruous boils,
Or like that scum, which, by need's lawless law
Enforced, Sanserra's starved men did draw
From parboiled shoes, and boots, and all the rest
Which were with any sovereign fatness blessed,
And like vile lying stones in saffroned tin,
Or warts, or weals, they hang upon her skin.
Round as the world's her head, on every side,
Like to the fatal ball which fell on Ide,
Or that whereof God had such jealousy,
As for the ravishing thereof we die.
Thy head is like a rough-hewn statue of jet,
Where marks for eyes, nose, mouth, are yet scarce set;
Like the first Chaos, or flat seeming face
Of Cynthia, when th' earth's shadows her embrace.

Illustrations

Images of John Donne.

Portrait of John Donne, c. 1595,
National Portrait Gallery, London

Portrait of John Donne at Deanery, St Paul's, 1622

Portrait of John Donne, 1630

John Donne, 1610

John Donne, St Paul's Cathedral

John Donne by Nigel Boonhma, 2012

A NOTE ON JOHN DONNE

John Donne was, Robert Graves said, a 'Muse poet', a poet who wrote passionately of the Muse. It is easy to see Donne as a love poet, in the tradition of love poets such as Bernard de Ventadour, Dante, Petrarch, Cavalcanti, Maurice Scève and Torquato Tasso. Donne has written his fair share of erotic poems. There is the bawdy allusions to the phallus in 'The Flea', while 'The Comparison' parodies the Petrarchan adoration poem, with references to the 'sweat drops of my mistress' breast'. Like Shakespeare in his parody sonnet 'My mistress' eyes are nothing like the sun',[1] Donne sends up the Petrarchan and courtly love genre with gross comparisons ('Like spermatic issue of ripe menstruous boils'). In 'The Bait', there is the archetypal Renaissance opening line 'Come live with me, and be my love', as used by Marlowe and Shakespeare, among others. And there is the complex, ambivalent eroticism of 'The Extasie', a much celebrated poem, and the 19th 'Elegy', where comes his famous couplet:

Licence my roving hands, and let them go
Before, behind, between, above, below.

Helen Gardner writes of 'The Extasie:

---

[1] See Lorna Hutson: "Why the Lady's Eyes Are Nothing Like the Sun", in Isobel Armstrong, ed: *New Feminist Discourses,* Routledge 1992, 154-175; Valerie Wayne, ed: *The Matter of Difference: Materialist Feminist Criticism of Shakespeare*, Harvester Wheatsheaf, 1991

* 73

There is no short poem of comparable merit over which such completely different views have been expressed, and no lover of Donne's poetry can be happy to leave the question in its present state of deadlock. For it is obvious that those who assert that the poem is the supreme expression of Donne's 'philosophy of love' and those who declare that it is a quasi-dramatic piece of special pleading have now no hope of converting each other.2

Donne's love poems are typical love poems, running through the gamut of emotions from desire through sex to loathing and loss and, as ever in Western poetry, death.3 'The justification of natural love as fullness of joy and life is the deepest thought in Donne's love-poems' writes Herbert Grierson.4 The *Songs and Sonnets* celebrate the many faceted emotions of love, emotions that are so familiar in love poetry from Sappho to Adrienne Rich. Louis Martz says 'the *Song and sonnets* hold within themselves every conceivable attitude toward love threatened by change'.5 Well, Donne does not quite cover *every* emotion of love, but a good deal of them. In 'The Canonization' we find the age-old Neoplatonic belief that two can become as one ('we two being one', or 'we shall/ Be one', he writes in 'Lovers' Infiniteness'), a common belief in love poetry. In 'The legacy', Donne proposes another

---

2 In "The Argument about *The Ecstasy*", in H. Davis & Helen Gardner, eds: *Elizabethan and Jacobean Studies Presented to F.P. Wilson*, Clarendon Press, Oxford 1959; M.Y. Hughes: "Some of Donne's "Ecstasies"", *Public-ations of the Modern Language Association of America*, Clarendon Press, Oxford 1959; M.Y. Hughes: "The Lineage of *The Ecstasy*, *Modern Language Review*, XXVII, 1932, 1-5.

3 See Claude J. Summers & Ted-Larry Pebworth, eds: *The Eagle and the Dove: Reassessing John Donne*, University of Missouri Press, Columbia 1986; P. Crutwell: "The Love Poetry of John Donne", in M. Bradbury & D.Palmer, eds: *Metaphysical Poetry*, Arnold 1970; John A. Clair: "Donne's 'The Canonization'", *Publications of the Modern Language Association of America*, vol. LXX, 1965, 300-2; J. Bennett: The Love Poetry of John Donne, in J. Dover Wilson, ed: *Seventeenth Century Studies Presented to Sir Herbert Grierson*, Clarendon Press, Oxford 1938

4 Quoted in Julian Lovelock, ed, 219

5 Louis Martz: *The Wit of Love*, Notre Dame, 1969

common belief – that love for lovers can last an eternity, even though it only lasts an hour or so of external, public, chronological time: 'lovers' hours be full eternity'. In Shakespeare *Sonnets* we find the same concentration on time, on the relation between time and love. Much of Donne's love poetry looks back from the vantage point of old age, as in Thomas Hardy or C.P. Cavafy. 'Love's Alchemy' offers ironic commentaries on the beliefs of the alchemical powers of love which seems to be alchemical glorifying 'elixir', but turns out to be, more often, 'odoriferous':

> So, lovers dream a rich and long delight,
> But get a winter-seeming summer night.

The *Songs and Sonnets* tell the story of love from the viewpoint of a talented, ironic, detached-yet-passionately-involved artist, someone, like Petrarch or Giraut de Borneil, very conscious of how he presents himself in poetry. Always in Donne, as in other love poets, self-consciousness comes to the fore. For in talking of love, Donne is, like Petrarch or Guinicelli, also talking of himself. Indeed, Petrarch's *Rime Sparse* reads as a series of poetic meditations upon the poet's self-in-love: it is the same with John Donne. The *Songs and Sonnets* describe love, yes, but also, rather, how love affects one particular person, how love is experienced by one person, how love is mediated through the rigorous forms of poetry. 'Yet, love and hate me too,' the poet tells his beloved in 'The Prohibition', loving the drama of love, loving to dramatize his love, loving the idea of loving-unto-death, as in the myths of Tristan and Isolde or Anthony and Cleopatra ('Love me, that I may die the gentler way' he implores his lover). Yet in speaking of his beloved, he speaks, really, of himself. Donne's love poetry, like (nearly) all love poetry, is self-reflexive. Although he would 'ne'er parted be', as he writes in 'Song: Sweetest love, I do not go', he knows, too, that love poetry comes out of loss. The beloved woman is not there, so art takes her place. The *Songs and Sonnets* arise from loss, loss of love; they take the place of love. For, if he were clasping his beloved in those feverish embraces as described in 'The Extasie' and 'Elegy', he would not, obviously, bother with poetry. Love poetry has this ambivalent, difficult relationship with love. The poetry is not love, and is no real substitute for it. And writing of love exacerbates the pain and insecurity of the experience of love. The poetry of love becomes vanity (albeit highly sophisticated vanity). Vanity, certainly, is one of the major 'hidden agendas' of the great love poems of the West – Petrarch's *Canzoniere*, Scève's *Délie*, Shakespeare's *Sonnets*, du Bellay's *Sonnets For Helen* and Dante's *Vita Nuova*.

John Donne's poetry is marked by *wit*, by an incisive explorative imagination. Donne is certainly humorous; he parodies existing poetic forms and styles; he is conscious of the foolish positions lovers put themselves in when they concentrate on love to the exclusion of everything else. And Donne produces not a few very memorable poetic moments, not least in that incredible opening to the 'Song', where he writes:

Go, and catch a falling star,
  Get with child a mandrake root...

This is a truly wonderful opening of a poem. It must have come to him straight away, out of nowhere, or, rather, straight from the Muse. While 'catching a falling star' may not be too out-of-the-ordinary, 'getting a mandrake root with child' is far more startling. Of course, in the Renaissance era, talk of the magical properties of herbs and plants, talk of witchcraft and healing and the hallucinogenic qualities of *mandragora* was not so unusual as at other times. In our contemporary era, mandrakes are not unknown, for there has been a revival of interest in all things occult, New Age and praeternatural. Even so, Donne's lines are still startling. Those two lines leap at you with total authority, and total quirkiness. The opening establishes itself instantly, and idiosyncratically, like that other quirky line, Before, behind, between, above, below.'

Like Petrarch, Donne is a self-conscious poet who is aware of forming a poetic persona in his poetry. His *Epithalamions*, for instance, are quite different Spenser's marriage songs. Spenser sings breathlessly and lyrically about the promises of love awaiting the couple. Donne is more circumspect, building into his nuptial celebrations hints of disillusion and death. Donne has a piquant death-consciousness, not only apparent in his many *Elegies* for dead people. Spenser too wrote elegies, but Donne's *Elegies* are filled with what we might call a 'modern' awareness of death, with something exhausted, dejected and depressed in it, beyond the usual sorrow and mourning found in, say, Spenser's *Elegies*. Donne's death-consciousness knows the vanity of feeding on 'supernatural food', religion, as he calls it in 'The First Anniversary', *An Anatomy of the World*.

Donne does not keep still: his heightened sense of irony, wit and humour do not allow him to keep still. He cannot be reduced to one viewpoint. Like Shakespeare, Donne is slippery, psychologically, ontologically, metaphysically. The never-ending dialectic of his poetry is expressed in the many contradictions in his lines, as statement is followed by counter-statement, much as in Samuel Beckett. Donne arrives at where he is 'through a series of negatives', to use Lawrence Durrell's phrase. Like Gide, like Petrarch, like the courtly love poets, Donne is not so much in love with love but in love with the poetry of love, with the debate and argument of love. The philosophical slipperiness of Donne's poetry is also expressed in his visual imagery: 'The Extasie', writes Thomas Docherty, one of the best of recent Donne commentators, 'abounds in spatial confusions of the lovers it attempts to describe and circumscribe, with their eye beams crossing, hands cemented, bodies intertwined and so on.' (77) Donne will happily change the gender of the speaker of a poem, or move from a subjective, first person viewpoint to a third person, distanced viewpoint.

A poem that illustrates Donne's brilliant dialectical poesie is found in one of his best poems, 'Upon the Annunciation and Passion Falling Upon One Day, 1608'. Donne is very simple in this poem, which is usually a good start in poetry. Simple and clear. Today, says the narrator, 'My soul eats twice'. He goes on to explore the ambiguities that arise when the moment that the Son of God is conceived in the womb of the Blessed Virgin Mary, on 25 March, Lady Day, the Annunciation, occurs at the same moment that Christ is crucified. Again and again in the poem, Donne investigates how it is that Christ comes into the world and is taken away immediately: 'Christ hither and away...Christ came, and went away'. The simultaneous Annunciation and Passion on 25 March suggests the age-old Western love-death to Donne the Metaphysical poet. For him, the joint Annunciation and Passion of Christianity conjoins the moment of orgasmic joy, the glory of birth, with the moment of intense suffering, the glory of pain. The two moments represent, for Donne, the twin poles of existence:

birth and death, or love and death. The Alpha and Omega of life, for Donne, is this love—death duality (or union), like the *yin—yang* dualism in Chinese religion, or the *shiva—shakti* dualism in Hindu religion. Throughout his poetry Donne plays with opposites such as active/ passive, in/ out, hot/ cold, soul/ body, light/ dark, sadness/ ecstasy, sacred/ secular, old/ young, love/ death. These are the basic opposites, or pairs, of poetry. Petrarch employed them profusely, with his 'conceits', those ice/ fire images which were so influential in European poetry. A. E. Dyson and Julian Lovelock speak of 'the extraordinary intensity and deviousness of his conceits'.[6] Donne is similarly Petrarchan, and in 'Upon the Annunciation and Passion Falling Upon One Day, 1608', he sees in the fusion of the Annunciation and Passion the ontological poles of life, where 'first and last concur' as he puts it (see page 33). He makes the dichotomies visual, too, he crystallizes the ambiguities with powerful visual images:

Sad and rejoiced she 'seen at once, and
At almost fifty, and at scarce fifteen.

The twin poles of ontology are given different names by Donne, as they are by poets throughout their careers. In Donne sometimes it is being/ non-being, or love/ death, or time/ timelessness. The mystical side of Donne is a powerful undercurrent in his love poetry. In 'The Canonization' he explores the relation of love to time, something that greatly vexed Shakespeare, and which was a major theme of the Sonnets. 'We are tapers too, and at our own cost die' says Donne, hitting the mark in just one line. All we have to do, the narrator tells his beloved, in poem after poem, is *realize*. Realize what exactly? *It.* What? 'we two being one, are it' says Donne. The nowness of life, really, Donne says. The timeless moment, as T. S. Eliot called it in his *Four Quartets*. The moment that is *now*, and *here*. This is ever the aim of mysticism, this ache for the 'two-in-oneness', as Thomas Hardy termed it in *Jude the Obscure*.

There is a good case for seeing Donne as a Muse-orientated poet, a poet who glorifies 'the feminine', in women, and in poetic abstractions. 'O fair love, love's impetuous rage,/ Be my true mistress still' he writes in 'Elegy 16: *On His Mistress*.

6 Dyson & Lovelock: "Contracted Thus: 'The Sunne Rising', in Lovelock, ed, 191

He adores women, certainly ('what a miracle she was', he writes in 'The Relic'). Donne's relationship to women is ambivalent, as in Shakespeare or Petrarch.[7] Simultaneously he loves and loathes them. Love and hate exist in a continuum in Donne's mythopoeia of emotion. Studies can be written, and have been written, about Donne's religious sensibilities, about his relation to the Madonna, and to the 'Virgin Queen' of the era, Queen Elizabeth I.[8]

It is easy to rewrite 'John Donne' as a religious poet. By 'rewrite' we mean to 'read' Donne as a religious poet. Indeed, he is often viewed in this way, as one of the 'metaphysical poets' (George Herbert, Richard Crashaw, Henry Vaughan, Thomas Traherne). In the *Holy Sonnets* and *Divine Meditations* Donne comes across as a deeply yearning but also deeply critical religious poet, someone who discourses at

---

[7] See, for instance, on Donne, women, eroticism and the Renaissance: Mary Beth Rose, ed: *Women in the Middle Ages and the Renaissance*, Syracuse University Press 1986; Maurer Marget: "The Real Presence of Lucy Russell, Countess of Bedford, and the Terms of John Donne's "Honour is so sublime Perfection", *English Literary History,* XLVII, 1980, 205-35; Ian Maclean: *The Renaissance Notion of Woman*, Cambridge University Press 1985; Stevie Davies: *The idea of Woman in Renaissance literature: The Feminine Reclaimed*, harvester Press, Brighton 1986; Virginia Ramey Molenkott: "John Donne and the limitations of Androgyny", *Journal of English and Germanic Philology*, LXXX, 1981, 22-38; Lindsay Mann: "The typology of Woman in Donne's *Anniversaries*", *Renaissance and Reformation*, 1987, 37-350; David Novarr: *The Disinterred Muse: Donne's Texts and Contexts*, Cornell University Press 1980; Linda Woodbridge: *Women and the English Renaissance: Literature and the Nature of Womankind 1540-1620*, University of Illinois Press, Urbana 1984; R.V. Young: "O my America, my new-found land": Pornography and Imperial Politics in Donne's Elegies", *SC Review*, IV, 1987, 35-48; Lisa Jardine, ed: *Still Harping on Daughters: Women and Drama in the Age of Shakespeare*, Harvester Wheatsheaf 1983; Marianne L. Novy: *Love's Arguments: Gender relations in Shakespeare*, University of North Carolina, Chapel 1984;

[8] See Helen Gardner, James Whinny; Julian Lovelock; Carole Levin: "Power, politics, and sexuality: images of Elizabeth I", in Jean R. Brink et al, eds: *The Politics of Gender in Early Modern, Sixteenth Century Studies and Essays*, 12, 1989, 95-110; Leonard Tennenhouse: *Power on Display: The Politics of Shakespeare's Genres*, Methuen 1986; Roy Strong: *The Cult of Elizabeth I*, Thames & Hudson 1977; Peter Stallybrass: "Patriarchal territories", in M. Ferguson et al, eds: *Rewriting the Renaissance*, University of Chicago Press, Chicago 1986, 123-142

length on 'the progress of the soul', while at the same time criticizing both the 'progress' itself and his writing about this 'progress'.[9] This simultaneous exalting and criticizing makes Donne 'modern', though the courtly love poets had cursed themselves for loving, and for writing about love, thus making the pain of love worse. In Donne's religious poems, the usual concerns of traditional Christianity - pain, flesh, lust, death, corruption, punishment, sin, etc - are given a vigorous going over. The *Divine Meditations* abound in extreme emotions - we are constantly reminded of 'joy', 'pain', 'poison', 'doom', 'weeping', 'grief', 'hell', 'sickness' and 'sin'. These are the terms that fill up the *Divine Meditations*. In them religious poems, Donne takes on the great themes of theology and explores with a relentless energy. The two things, though, love and religion, are part of the same experience for Donne, as for so many artists. The passion of love and the passion of God are the sensual and sacred sides of the same phenomena, which is life. The *Songs and Sonnets* are the secular aspect of the existential experience of being alive; the *Holy Sonnets* are the religious dimension. The sacred and profane series of poems pivot around the poet. For what concerns Donne is how love and religion relate to him, to his 'black soul', as he puts it in the fourth of the *Divine Meditations*.

---

[9] See Earl Miner: *The Metaphysical Mode from Donne to Cowley*, Princeton University Press, New jersey 1970; D.L. Peterson: "John Donne's *Holy Sonnets* and the Anglican Doctrine of Contrition", *Studies in Philology*, LVI, 1959, 504-18; F.A. Rowe: *I laugh at Paradise*, Epworth Press 1964; R. Tuve: *Elizabethan and Metaphysical Imagery*, University of Chicago Press 1947; R.L. Colie: "The Rhetoric of Transcendence", *Philological Quarterly*, XLIII, 1964, 145-70; Barbara Kiefer Lewalski: *Protestant Poetics and the Seventeenth Century Religious Lyric*, Princeton University Press, New Jersey, 1979; Dennis Flynn: "Donne's Catholicism: I & II", *Recusant History*, XIII, 1975-6, 1-17, 178-95; Marius Beley: "Religious Cynicism in Donne's Poetry", *Kenyon Review*, XIV, 1952, 619-46

SELECT BIBLIOGRAPHY

N.J.C. Andreasen: *John Donne, Conservative Revolutionary*, Princeton University Press, New Jersey 1967
R.C. Bald: *John Donne: A Life*, Clarendon Press 1970
Ilona Bell: "The Role of the Lady in Donne's *Songs and Sonnets*", *Studies in English Literature*, vol. XXIII, 1983, 113-129
Louis I. Bredvold: *The Religious Thought of Donne in Relation to Medieval and Later Tradition*, Macmillan, New York 1925
John Carey: *John Donne: Life, Mind and Art*, Faber 1981
Charles Monroe Coffin: *John Donne and the New Philosophy*, Columbia University Press, New York 1937
Thomas Docherty: *John Donne, Undone*, Methuen 1986
John Donne: *The Complete English Poems*, ed. A.J. Smith, Penguin 1971
—*Sermons*, eds: G. R. Potter & E.M. Simpson, University of California Press, Berkeley, 1953-62
—*The Elegies and the Songs and Sonnets*, ed Helen Gardner, Clarendon Press 1965
William Empsom: "Donne the space man", *Kenyon Review*, 19, 1957, 337-99
Helen Gardner, ed: *John Donne: A Collection of Critical Essays*, Prentice-Hall, N.J. 1962
Helen Gardner, ed: *John Donne: A Collection of Critical Essays*, Prentice-Hall, New Jersey 1962
Donald L. Guss: *John Donne, Petrarchist*, Wayne State University Press, Detroit 1966;
Marritt Y. Hughes: "Some of Donne's "Ecstasies"", *PMLA*, vol LXXV, 1960, 509-18
Pierre Legouis: *Donne the Craftsman*, Russell & Russell, New York 1962
J.B. Leishman: *The Monarch of Wit*, Hutchinson 1951
Julian Lovelock, ed: *Songs and Sonnets: A Casebook*, Macmillan 1973
Arthur F. Marotti: *John Donne, Coterie Poet*, University of Wisconsin

Press, Madison 1986

Earl Miner: *The Metaphysical Mode from Donne to Cowley*, Princeton University Press, New York 1969

Una Nelly: *The Poet Donne*, Cork University Press, Cork 1969

David Novarr: *The Disinterred Muse Donne's Texts and Contexts*, Cornell University Press 1980

A.C. Partridge: *John Donne: Language and Style*, Andre Deutsch 1978

Maureen Sabine: *Feminine Engendered Faith: The Poetry of John Donne and Richard Crashaw*, Macmillan 1992

Wilbur Sanders: *John Donne's Poetry, Cambridge University Press 1971*

Terry G. Sherwood: *Fulfilling the circle: A Study of John Donne's Thought*, University of Toronto Press 1984

A.J. Smith, ed: *John Donne: The Critical Heritage*, Routledge & Kegan Paul 1975

P.G. Stanwood & Heather Ross Assals, eds: *John Donne and the Theology of Language*, University Press of Columbia 1986

Gary Stringer, ed: *New Essays on Donne*, Universitat Salzburg 1977

James Winny: *A Preface to Donne*, Longman 1970

Beauties, Beasts, and Enchantment

CLASSIC FRENCH FAIRY TALES

Translated and with an Introduction by Jack Zipes

A collection of 36 classic French fairy tales translated by renowned writer Jack Zipes. *Cinderella*, *Beauty and the Beast*, *Sleeping Beauty* and *Little Red Riding Hood* are among the classic fairy tales in this amazing book.
Includes illustrations from fairy tale collections.
Jack Zipes has written and published widely on fairy tales.

'Terrific... a succulent array of 17th and 18th century 'salon' fairy tales'
- *The New York Times Book Review*

'These tales are adventurous, thrilling in a way fairy tales are meant to be... The translation from the French is modern, happily free of archaic and hyperbolic language... a fine and sophisticated collection' - *New York Tribune*

'Enjoyable to read... a unique collection of French regional folklore' - *Library Journal*

'Charming stories accompanied by attractive pen-and-ink drawings' - *Chattanooga Times*

Introduction and illustrations   612pp.   ISBN 9781861712510 Pbk   ISBN 9781861713193 Hbk

Arseny Tarkovsky

translated and edited by Virginia Rounding

Arseny Tarkovsky is the neglected Russian poet, father of the acclaimed film director Andrei Tarkovsky. This new book gathers together many of Tarkovsky's most lyrical and heartfelt poems, in Rounding's clear, new translations. Many of Tarkovsky's poems appeared in his son's films, such as *Mirror, Stalker, Nostalghia* and *The Sacrifice*. There is an introduction by Rounding, and a bibliography of both Arseny and Andrei Tarkovsky.

Bibliography and notes 124pp 3rd ed ISBN 9781861712660 Hbk ISBN 9781861711144

In the Dim Void

Samuel Beckett's Late Trilogy: *Company, Ill Seen, Ill Said* and *Worstward Ho*

by Gregory Johns

This book discusses the luminous beauty and dense, rigorous poetry of Samuel Beckett's late works, *Company, Ill Seen, Ill Said* and *Worstward Ho*. Gregory Johns looks back over Beckett's long writing career, charting the development from the *Molloy-Malone Dies-Unnamable* trilogy through the 'fizzles' of the 1960s to the elegiac lyricism of the *Company* series. Johns compares the trilogy with late plays such as *Ghosts, Footfalls* and *Rockaby*.

Bibliography, notes. Illustrated. 120pp
ISBN 9781861712974 Pbk and ISBN 9781861712608 Hbk
9781861713407 E-book

Thomas A. Christie

JOHN HUGHES
& EIGHTIES CINEMA
Teenage Hopes & American Dreams

John Hughes (1950-2009) is one of the best-loved figures in 1980s American filmmaking, and considered by many to be among the finest and most celebrated comedy writers of his generation. His memorable motion pictures are insightful, humanistic, culturally aware, and paint a vibrant picture of the United States in a decade of rapid social and political change.

Bibliography, notes, illustrations   372pp.
ISBN 9781861713896 Pbk   ISBN 9781861713988 Hbk
Also available: *Ferris Bueller's Day Off: Pocket Movie Guide*

CRESCENT MOON PUBLISHING

web: www.crmoon.com e-mail: cresmopub@yahoo.co.uk

ARTS, PAINTING, SCULPTURE

The Art of Andy Goldsworthy
Andy Goldsworthy: Touching Nature
Andy Goldsworthy in Close-Up
Andy Goldsworthy: Pocket Guide
Andy Goldsworthy In America
Land Art: A Complete Guide
The Art of Richard Long
Richard Long: Pocket Guide
Land Art In the UK
Land Art in Close-Up
Land Art In the U.S.A.
Land Art: Pocket Guide
Installation Art in Close-Up
Minimal Art and Artists In the 1960s and After
Colourfield Painting
Land Art DVD, TV documentary
Andy Goldsworthy DVD, TV documentary
The Erotic Object: Sexuality in Sculpture From Prehistory to the Present Day
Sex in Art: Pornography and Pleasure in Painting and Sculpture
Postwar Art
Sacred Gardens: The Garden in Myth, Religion and Art
Glorification: Religious Abstraction in Renaissance and 20th Century Art
Early Netherlandish Painting
Leonardo da Vinci
Piero della Francesca
Giovanni Bellini
Fra Angelico: Art and Religion in the Renaissance
Mark Rothko: The Art of Transcendence
Frank Stella: American Abstract Artist
Jasper Johns
Brice Marden
Alison Wilding: The Embrace of Sculpture
Vincent van Gogh: Visionary Landscapes
Eric Gill: Nuptials of God
Constantin Brancusi: Sculpting the Essence of Things
Max Beckmann
Caravaggio
Gustave Moreau
Egon Schiele: Sex and Death In Purple Stockings
Delizioso Fotografico Fervore: Works In Process 1
Sacro Cuore: Works In Process 2
The Light Eternal: J.M.W. Turner
The Madonna Glorified: Karen Arthurs

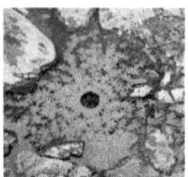

LITERATURE

J.R.R. Tolkien: The Books, The Films, The Whole Cultural Phenomenon
J.R.R. Tolkien: Pocket Guide
Tolkien's Heroic Quest
The *Earthsea* Books of Ursula Le Guin
Beauties, Beasts and Enchantment: Classic French Fairy Tales
German Popular Stories by the Brothers Grimm
Philip Pullman and *His Dark Materials*
Sexing Hardy: Thomas Hardy and Feminism
Thomas Hardy's *Tess of the d'Urbervilles*
Thomas Hardy's *Jude the Obscure*
Thomas Hardy: The Tragic Novels
Love and Tragedy: Thomas Hardy
The Poetry of Landscape in Hardy
Wessex Revisited: Thomas Hardy and John Cowper Powys
Wolfgang Iser: Essays and Interviews
Petrarch, Dante and the Troubadours
Maurice Sendak and the Art of Children's Book Illustration
Andrea Dworkin
Cixous, Irigaray, Kristeva: The *Jouissance* of French Feminism
Julia Kristeva: Art, Love, Melancholy, Philosophy, Semiotics and Psychoanalysis
Hélène Cixous I Love You: The *Jouissance* of Writing
Luce Irigaray: Lips, Kissing, and the Politics of Sexual Difference
Peter Redgrove: Here Comes the Flood
Peter Redgrove: Sex-Magic-Poetry-Cornwall
Lawrence Durrell: Between Love and Death, East and West
Love, Culture & Poetry: Lawrence Durrell
Cavafy: Anatomy of a Soul
German Romantic Poetry: Goethe, Novalis, Heine, Hölderlin
Feminism and Shakespeare
Shakespeare: Love, Poetry & Magic
The Passion of D.H. Lawrence
D.H. Lawrence: Symbolic Landscapes
D.H. Lawrence: Infinite Sensual Violence
Rimbaud: Arthur Rimbaud and the Magic of Poetry
The Ecstasies of John Cowper Powys
Sensualism and Mythology: The Wessex Novels of John Cowper Powys
Amorous Life: John Cowper Powys and the Manifestation of Affectivity (H.W. Fawkner)
Postmodern Powys: New Essays on John Cowper Powys (Joe Boulter)
Rethinking Powys: Critical Essays on John Cowper Powys
Paul Bowles & Bernardo Bertolucci
Rainer Maria Rilke
Joseph Conrad: *Heart of Darkness*
In the Dim Void: Samuel Beckett
Samuel Beckett Goes into the Silence
André Gide: Fiction and Fervour
Jackie Collins and the Blockbuster Novel
Blinded By Her Light: The Love-Poetry of Robert Graves
The Passion of Colours: Travels In Mediterranean Lands
Poetic Forms

POETRY

Ursula Le Guin: Walking In Cornwall
Peter Redgrove: Here Comes The Flood
Peter Redgrove: Sex-Magic-Poetry-Cornwall
Dante: Selections From the Vita Nuova
Petrarch, Dante and the Troubadours
William Shakespeare: Sonnets
William Shakespeare: Complete Poems
Blinded By Her Light: The Love-Poetry of Robert Graves
Emily Dickinson: Selected Poems
Emily Brontë: Poems
Thomas Hardy: Selected Poems
Percy Bysshe Shelley: Poems
John Keats: Selected Poems
Joh n Keats: Poems of 1820
D.H. Lawrence: Selected Poems
Edmund Spenser: Poems
Edmund Spenser: Amoretti
John Donne: Poems
Henry Vaughan: Poems
Sir Thomas Wyatt: Poems
Robert Herrick: Selected Poems
Rilke: Space, Essence and Angels in the Poetry of Rainer Maria Rilke
Rainer Maria Rilke: Selected Poems
Friedrich Hölderlin: Selected Poems
Arseny Tarkovsky: Selected Poems
Arthur Rimbaud: Selected Poems
Arthur Rimbaud: A Season in Hell
Arthur Rimbaud and the Magic of Poetry
Novalis: Hymns To the Night
German Romantic Poetry
Paul Verlaine: Selected Poems
Elizaethan Sonnet Cycles
D.J. Enright: By-Blows
Jeremy Reed: Brigitte's Blue Heart
Jeremy Reed: Claudia Schiffer's Red Shoes
Gorgeous Little Orpheus
Radiance: New Poems
Crescent Moon Book of Nature Poetry
Crescent Moon Book of Love Poetry
Crescent Moon Book of Mystical Poetry
Crescent Moon Book of Elizabethan Love Poetry
Crescent Moon Book of Metaphysical Poetry
Crescent Moon Book of Romantic Poetry
Pagan America: New American Poetry

MEDIA, CINEMA, FEMINISM and CULTURAL STUDIES

J.R.R. Tolkien: The Books, The Films, The Whole Cultural Phenomenon
J.R.R. Tolkien: Pocket Guide
The *Lord of the Rings* Movies: Pocket Guide
The Cinema of Hayao Miyazaki
Hayao Miyazaki: *Princess Mononoke*: Pocket Movie Guide
Hayao Miyazaki: *Spirited Away*: Pocket Movie Guide
Tim Burton : Hallowe'en For Hollywood
Ken Russell
Ken Russell: *Tommy*: Pocket Movie Guide
The Ghost Dance: The Origins of Religion
The Peyote Cult
Cixous, Irigaray, Kristeva: The *Jouissance* of French Feminism
Julia Kristeva: Art, Love, Melancholy, Philosophy, Semiotics and Psychoanalysis
Luce Irigaray: Lips, Kissing, and the Politics of Sexual Difference
Hélene Cixous I Love You: The *Jouissance* of Writing
Andrea Dworkin
'Cosmo Woman': The World of Women's Magazines
Women in Pop Music
HomeGround: The Kate Bush Anthology
Discovering the Goddess (Geoffrey Ashe)
The Poetry of Cinema
The Sacred Cinema of Andrei Tarkovsky
Andrei Tarkovsky: Pocket Guide
Andrei Tarkovsky: *Mirror*: Pocket Movie Guide
Andrei Tarkovsky: *The Sacrifice*: Pocket Movie Guide
Walerian Borowczyk: Cinema of Erotic Dreams
Jean-Luc Godard: The Passion of Cinema
Jean-Luc Godard: *Hail Mary*: Pocket Movie Guide
Jean-Luc Godard: *Contempt*: Pocket Movie Guide
Jean-Luc Godard: *Pierrot le Fou*: Pocket Movie Guide
John Hughes and Eighties Cinema
Ferris Bueller's Day Off: Pocket Movie Guide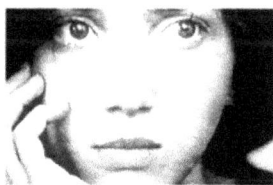
Jean-Luc Godard: Pocket Guide
The Cinema of Richard Linklater
Liv Tyler: Star In Ascendance
Blade Runner and the Films of Philip K. Dick
Paul Bowles and Bernardo Bertolucci
Media Hell: Radio, TV and the Press
An Open Letter to the BBC
Detonation Britain: Nuclear War in the UK
Feminism and Shakespeare
Wild Zones: Pornography, Art and Feminism
Sex in Art: Pornography and Pleasure in Painting and Sculpture
Sexing Hardy: Thomas Hardy and Feminism

The Light Eternal is a model monograph, an exemplary job. The subject matter of the book is beautifully organised and dead on beam. (Lawrence Durrell)
It is amazing for me to see my work treated with such passion and respect. (Andrea Dworkin)

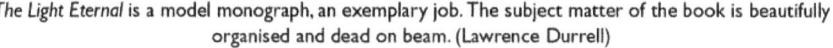

CRESCENT MOON PUBLISHING
P.O. Box 1312, Maidstone, Kent, ME14 5XU, Great Britain. www.crmoon.com

cresmopub@yahoo.co.uk   www.crescentmoon.org.uk

www.ingramcontent.com/pod-product-compliance
Lightning Source LLC
Chambersburg PA
CBHW061336040426
42444CB00011B/2958